THE HOUSE
WITH
NO DOOR
AFRICAN RIDDLE-POEMS

BRIAN SWANN

ILLUSTRATED BY
ASHLEY BRYAN

BROWNDEER PRESS
HARCOURT BRACE & COMPANY
San Diego   New York   London

To Roberta, with love
—B. S.

For dear friends
Richard and Martha Rowland
—A. B.

Library of Congress Cataloging-in Publication Data
Swann, Brian.
The house with no door: African riddle-poems/Brian Swann; illustrated by Ashley Bryan.
p.   cm.
"Browndeer Press."
Summary: A collection of original poems created from riddles of various African tribes.
ISBN 0-15-200805-5
1. Riddles—Adaptations—Juvenile poetry. 2. Folklore—Africa—Juvenile poetry.
3. Children's poetry, American. [1. Riddles—Adaptations. 2. Folklore—Africa.
3. American poetry.]I. Bryan, Ashley, ill. II. Title.
PS 3569.W 256 H6   1998
811'.54—dc20   95-43302

First edition
F E D C B A

Printed in Hong Kong

The illustrations in this book were done in tempera paints and
gouache on C. M. Fabriano 100/100 cotton paper.
The display type and text type were set in Neue Neuland.
Color separations by Bright Arts, Ltd., Hong Kong
Printed by South China Printing Company, Ltd., Hong Kong
This book was printed on totally chlorine-free Nymolla Matte Art paper.
Production supervision by Stanley Redfern and Pascha Gerlinger
Designed by Judythe Sieck

THE HOUSE
WITH
NO DOOR
AFRICAN RIDDLE-POEMS

The art on each left-hand page
contains the answer to the riddle.
If you look hard enough, you
may find other possible answers
included in the art.

(A strong hint of the answer appears on
each facing right-hand page.)

I have a house
that has no door.

I go everywhere with a person
who never lets me rest.

I stepped on it.
It stepped on me.

I make long journeys
flat on my back.

It is long, it is long, yet it
does not reach the tail of a donkey.

Trousers rolled to his knees,
the prince dashes about
in his many-colored coat
made without thread.

The spots are leaving.
They are going into hiding.

These are my children.
Let them stay behind
and be brought up properly.

The little chief from the north
sits rubbing his hands.
He says: Where I come from is good.
Where I go to is good.

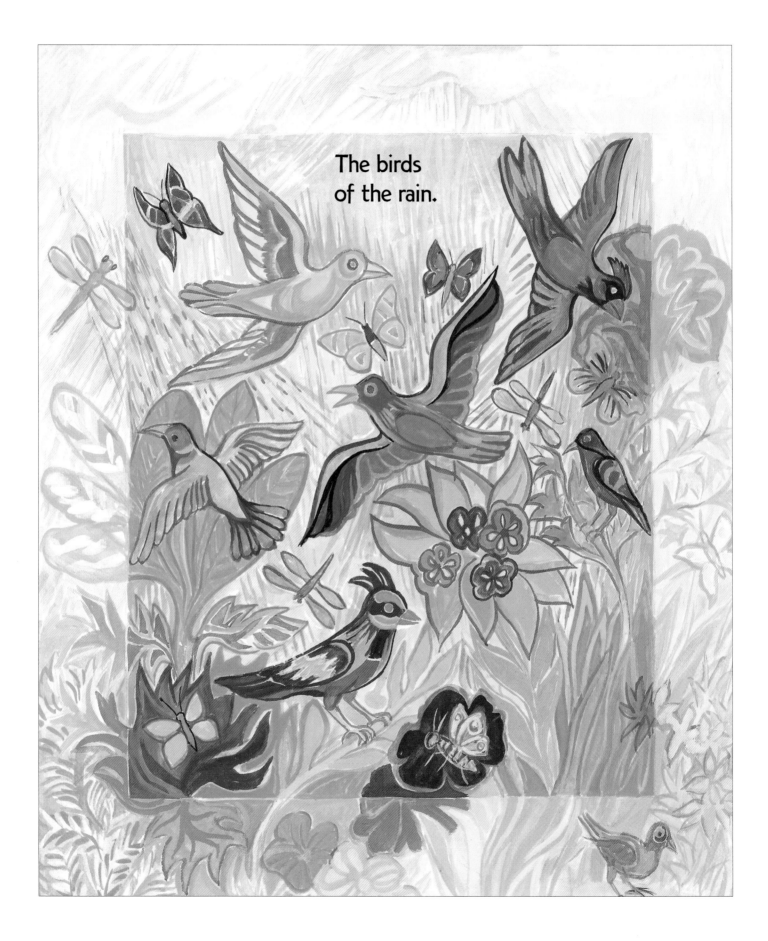

The birds
of the rain.

The white goats
are drifting
down
from the mountain.

Again she comes,
    the black girl.
She comes in the morning,
    the black girl.
In her mouth is a flute
    of red iron.
She comes dancing,
    the black girl.

I scattered my corn on the field.
It was gone the next day.

ANSWERS

Sometimes a riddle has more than one answer. Here are some possible answers to the riddles in this book.

egg

shadow

water

canoe

road

rooster

leopard

pumpkin

fly

butterflies

cup

snow

fire in the hearth

night sky with stars

ACKNOWLEDGMENTS

The riddles in this book are new poems based on the following sources.

Egg, water, snow, night sky with stars
G. Nakene, "Tlokwa Riddles," *African Studies* 1 (March 1943), northern Transvaal.

Shadow
Jack Glazier and Phyllis Gorfain Glazier, "Ambiguity and Exchange: The Double Dimension of Mbeere Riddles," *Journal of American Folklore* 89 (April-June 1976), Kenya.

Canoe, cup
D. F. Gowlett, "Some Lozi Riddles and Tongue-Twisters Annotated and Analysed," *African Studies* 25 (1966), Zambia.

Road
J. Bynon, "Riddle Telling among the Berbers of Central Morocco," *African Language Studies* VII (1967).

Rooster
P-D. Cole-Beuchat, "Riddles in Bantu," *African Studies* 16, no. 3 (1957), Ronga people, Ila, Zezura.

Leopard, pumpkin
Lyndon Harries, "Makua Song-Riddles from the Initiation Rites," *African Studies* 1 (1942), south Tanganyika and Portuguese East Africa.

Fly, fire in the hearth
Ernest Gray, "Some Riddles of the Nyanja People," *Bantu Studies* XIII (December 1939), Nyasaland.

Butterflies
L. Schapera, "Kxatla Riddles and Their Significance," *Bantu Studies* VI (September 1932), Bechuanaland.